What If We Are the Reflection?

Poetry Composed by Elizabeth Weseloh
Illustrated by Michelle Heitzner

What If We Are the Reflection?

Poetry Composed by Elizabeth Weseloh
Illustrated by Michelle Heitzner

Print copyright ©2021 by Elizabeth Weseloh and Michelle Heitzner
Cover art and illustrations copyright ©2021 by Elizabeth Weseloh and Michelle Heitnzer
All rights reserved. No part of this book, print or illustrations may be reproduced, scanned, stored, or distributed in any printed or electronic form without written permission from the author and/or illustrator.
ISBN: 9798510710465

Created with hope that the reader will develop an appreciation for the misunderstood psyche.

Possibly, you may not be able to suggest anything about the author that she has yet to consider herself.

Maiden Song

Grant the Sun her shine so bright.

I have been lost in the maze at least a fortnight.

Waiting for release from the shackles of fear.

Longing for love driving through a sphere.

As I glance out the window large,

My wonderment trembles, sinking the barge.

Will I be granted the freedom to see?

Or will all continue observation of me?

Sacrificial Lamb

Offering myself as sacrifice

For a world that turned it's back.

Once, twice, thrice,

Falling through a crack.

I do not wish for more than I am.

Yet, may be meant for more than I can.

Reaching out, calling a million names…

Response received: belief in a game.

Whom may it be that I need to call?

To steady this ship so none will fall.

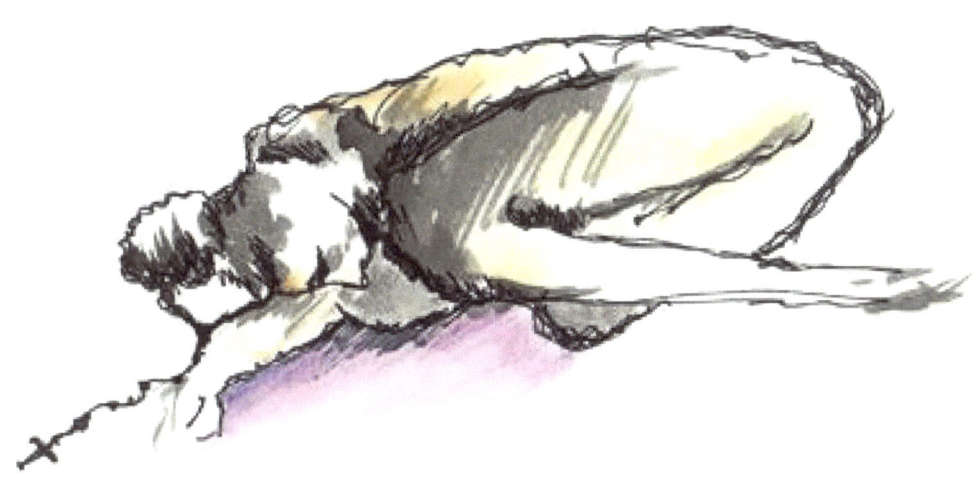

Forbidden Fruit

My eyes are open to the offer at hand.
To the dealer, I make my position stand.
The knowledge that broke the first time around,
Will not be released, to keep us aground.

Join and say: "I'll not take a bite."
These reptiles are tricky – continue to fight.
Remember the chance that is on the line.
Remember the one committing the crime.

Understand, you can change history for some.
Though, they must know, they cannot run.
We must face this issue with necks bent!
For now, eternity, do not give consent.

GAIA

She breathes in, breathes out.
    She chokes.
They doubt, you doubt.
    She croaks.
We know, we yell!
    She cries.
They push, we fell.
    She dies.
We fight, we win.
    She recovers.
You change, you are in.
    Her lovers.

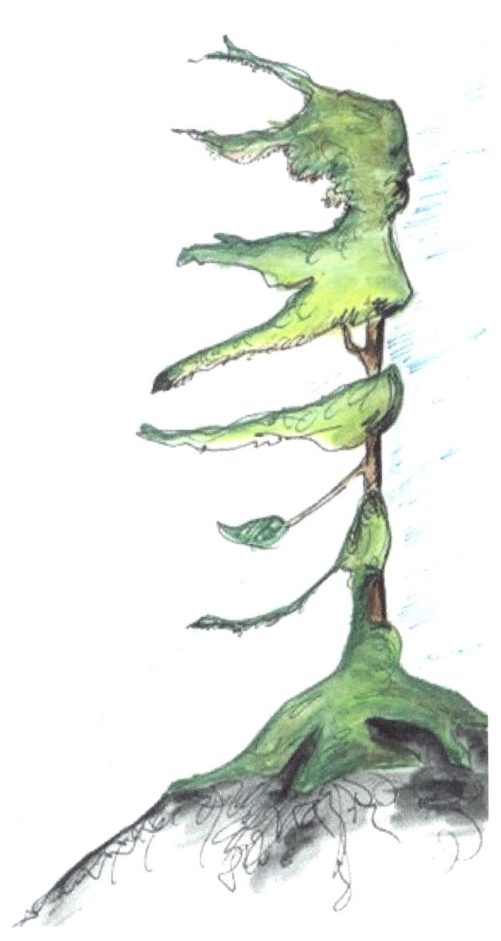

Reparation

On the left, I find the answers.
On the right, I find opposition.

I want to join the dancers.
Let the world know my position…

One does not only walk with Whole.
They can dance, skip, repair their soul.

A recommendation that all must see:
True worship is only on your knees.

Praise the Glory that brought you life.
Assist others, overcome strife.

Remember: Everyman has only one possession.
When the day arrives: cannot have recession.

Be giving of that which you have to all.
Your angel guarantees you will not fall.

Hope of Heaven

As the waves softly brush the shore,
My hair spreads, carrying thoughts before…
I dream of the day, far from now.
My pulse quickens, hope of somehow.
Yet, each day, pulls me farther apart.
That, which I knew, did depart.
My heart beats, pleading my core:
Please, Dear Destiny, bring it once more.

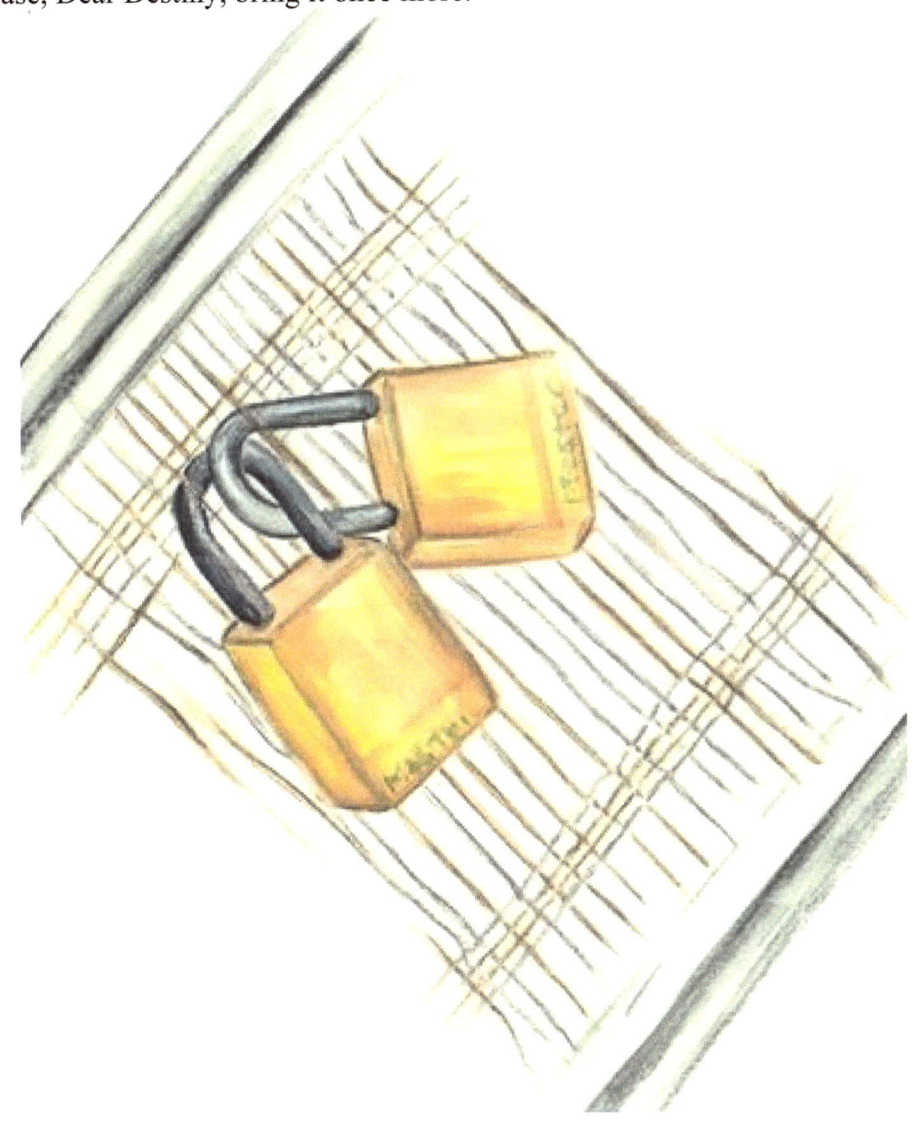

Faith Based

Of the one I called myself:
Forced to lay on that shelf…
For the reason behind your creation,
Placed your value into negation.
To devise your own without question?
Everyone knew your intention less than…
All to ensure your seeds were sown.
Following desires, itches, moans.
So, I was forced to turn to another.
There, my fears, quelled by My Brother.
It is not at all I no longer believe.
It is he, the cheater, that made me leave.

Exchange

On the tail of the wind, my ancestors call.
From the back of my mouth, my wisdom teeth awe.
How much longer will I have to wait?
I know, not prudent, to know the date.
Only two places I long to go…
One, if I choose, in a throw.
The step I must take before making the trip,
Depends on another, without a slip.
Hope for the best, look to the sky.
Promise, Dear Jupiter, not another lie.

Him

Did you think you touched me?
You never got that far.
Why is it you cannot see:
It was I who set the bar.

You want to bring me down?
You see how far I've come?
Remember who is listening.
Action cannot be undone.

Maybe, I do think of you.
Sorry, not fondly.
Pay attention to these rhymes,
You only touched my body.

I know it would bring pleasure.
To cause me pain.
But do you not even recall?
All I did sustain?

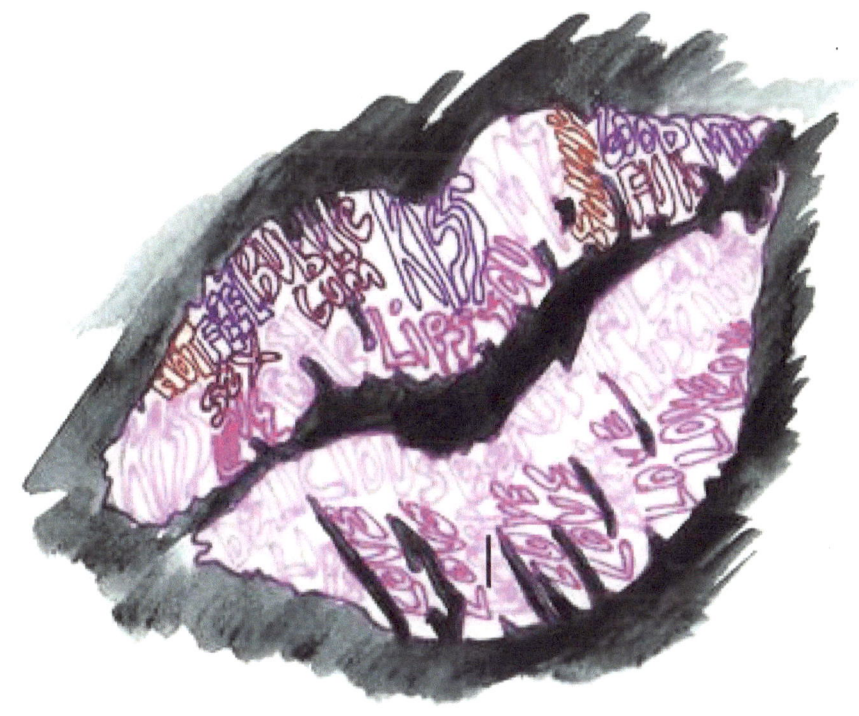

Psych

Lost in murky water.
Of my mind.
Genetics, environment,
So unkind.

I cleanse, I cleanse.
Cannot get clean.
Inner pain ails me,
Cannot be seen.

Inhale, inhale –
A deal was made?
Was there exchange?
A price now paid?

I pray, I pray.
This is my plight.
Psyching up:
One day, one fight.

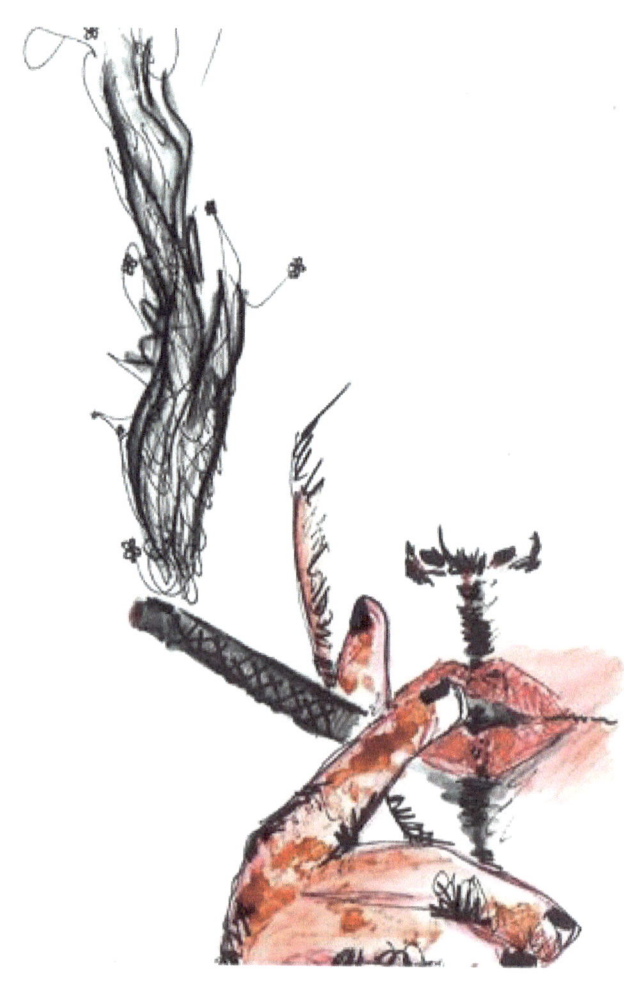

Doubt

Compose something "cheery"!
Is the critique.
This saddened heart.
Is the mystique.

There constantly.
A powerful ache.
This smile, my face,
A mask it makes.

So often, this pain,
Stabs deep, a knife.
Does my countenance
Reveal this strife?

Recommendation made:
Find the source.
I laugh, "My life!"
A powerful force.

I know it cannot,
Be really that bad…
Truly, I am not,
Always so sad.

Just, if you measure
The pleasure and pain…
From this doubt, I am sure,
You will refrain.

Maternal

The touch of her hand
Calms my nerves.

Her soothing voice
Always serves.

The ways I am like her
Make me smile.

Yet, somehow, they irk me
All the while.

It was her wit,
That hit you first.

Leaving you laughing, wondering,
Which is worse?

The way she held me…
Before I fall.

Creating need:
Give it my all.

Her laugh infectious,
Her smile serine.

Deserves to be placed
In a movie scene.

I hope she knows:
Her work is a success.

Not only upon I
Does she impress.

Love Forever,
Thanks abounding…

Nothing compared
To all my heart is sounding.

Trauma

My mind convinced
I am going to hell.
Though my soul
I did not sell.

Do everything I can
To be kind.
Still no solace
May I find?

You say I am saved?
Shh! Don't jinx it!
You say there's no hell?
SHH! Don't nix it!

I will rationalize it.
Because I am bad.
I cannot help all of this.
Because I am mad.

All I can do
Is confess, pray…
Over again, again
Each day.

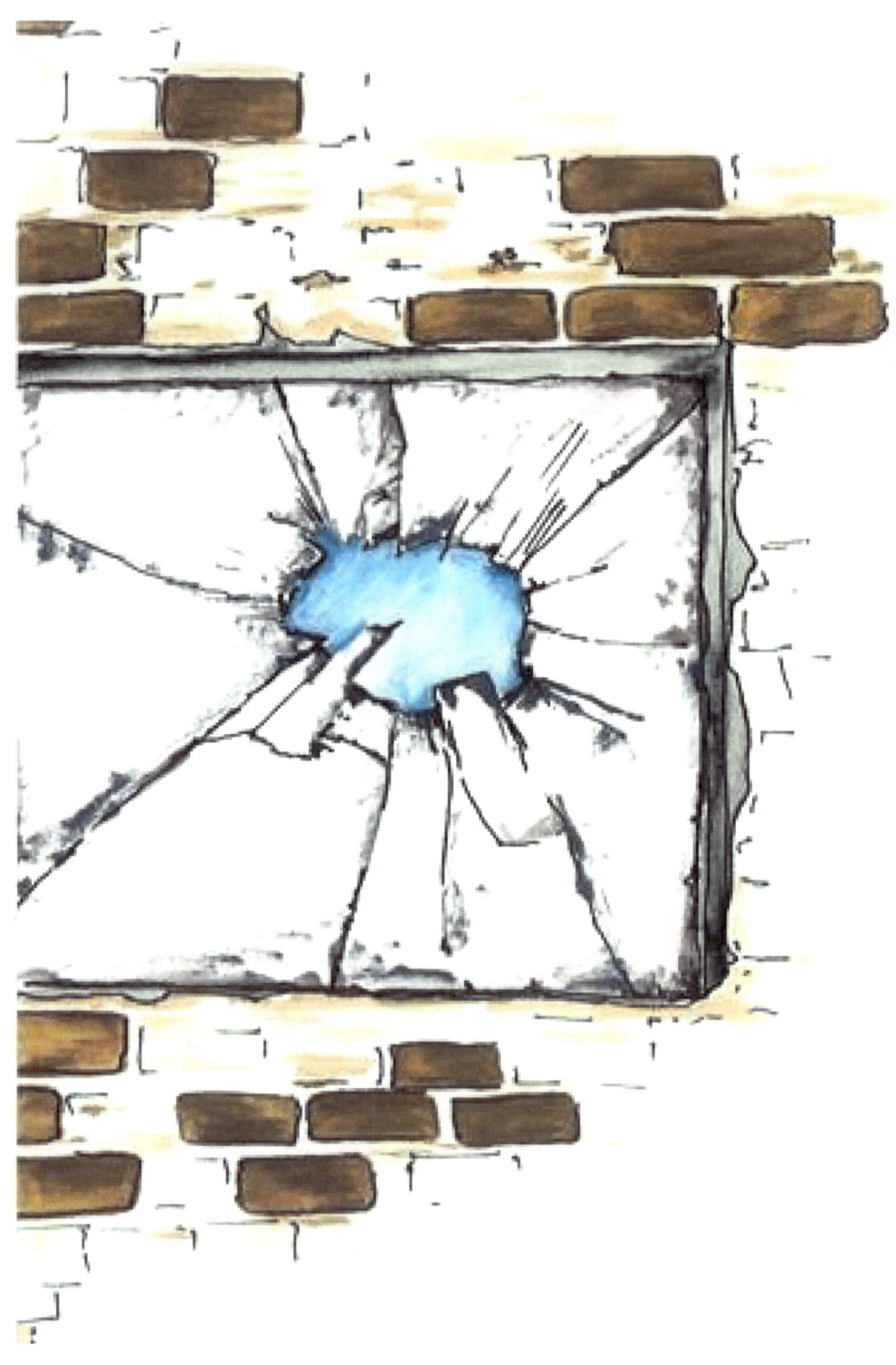

At Your Feet

I find my body alive.
With willingness to survive.

I need to be lifted up.
To share in His Cup.

I stare around the world,
Going out, hair curled:

I need this world to see:
Today, I feel I can be me.

Some days… something… holds me back.
Possibly due to all I lack.

As the day rolls on, insight I gain:
I feel, better thoughts, I can retain.

Please, keep the negative thoughts at bay.
At your feet, I continue to lay.

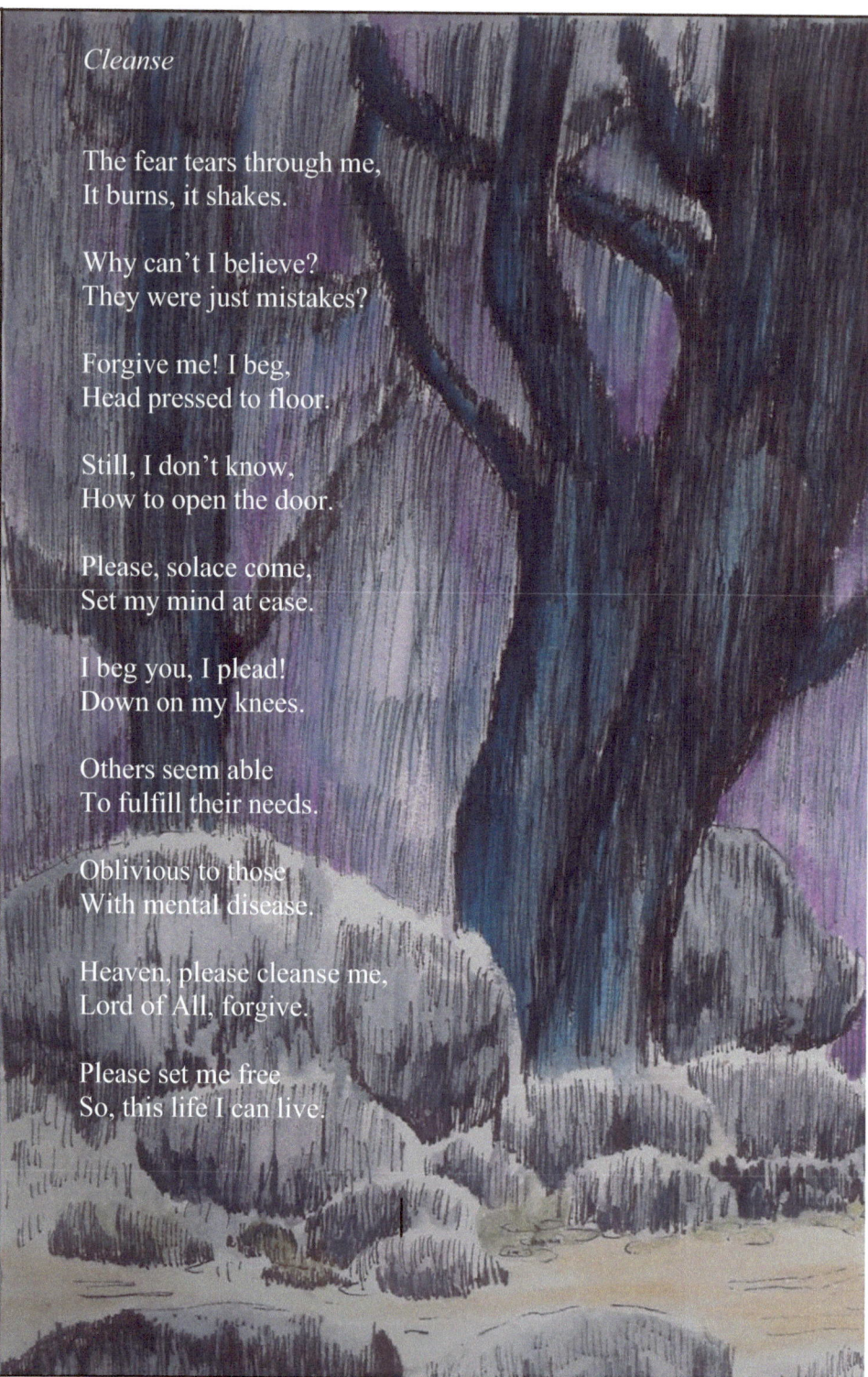

Cleanse

The fear tears through me,
It burns, it shakes.

Why can't I believe?
They were just mistakes?

Forgive me! I beg,
Head pressed to floor.

Still, I don't know,
How to open the door.

Please, solace come,
Set my mind at ease.

I beg you, I plead!
Down on my knees.

Others seem able
To fulfill their needs.

Oblivious to those
With mental disease.

Heaven, please cleanse me,
Lord of All, forgive.

Please set me free
So, this life I can live.

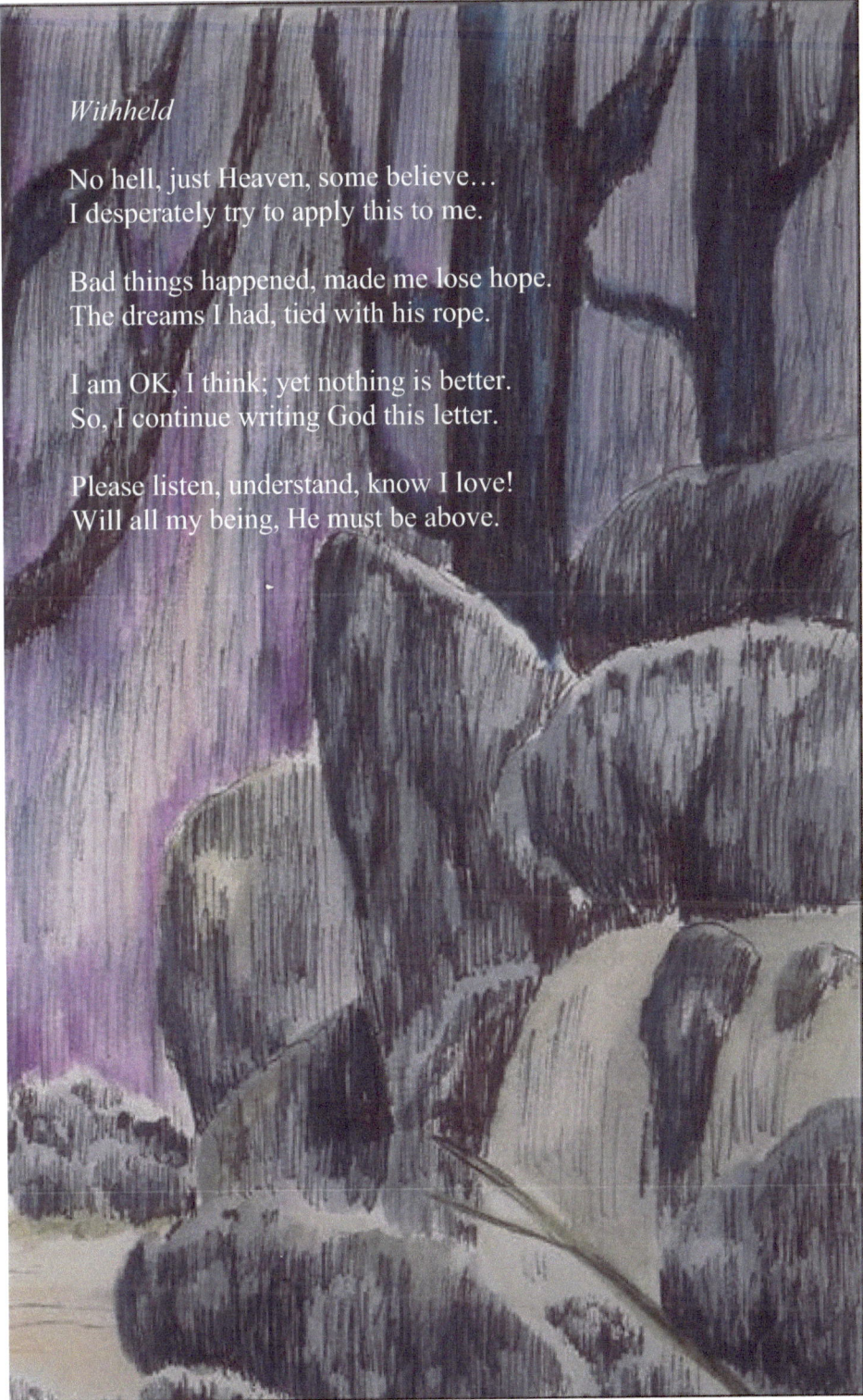

Withheld

No hell, just Heaven, some believe…
I desperately try to apply this to me.

Bad things happened, made me lose hope.
The dreams I had, tied with his rope.

I am OK, I think; yet nothing is better.
So, I continue writing God this letter.

Please listen, understand, know I love!
Will all my being, He must be above.

Absolute Discharge

Sit and wonder:
Is my mind my own?
Constantly fearful
To the flames I am thrown.
Tried to be all
I believed was right…
Still, I grapple:
Did I use my might?
Dates approaching.
Must stand strong…
Please God, please,
Let fear be wrong!
All I wanted
Was to be accepted.
Shamefully, I fear:
Ultimately rejected.
God, do you see?
Good inside?
Please God, give reason,
Not to hide.
I Praise You, Love You,
Worship You only!
Please, Lord, tell me,
I am not phony.

Faces

I am fearful of the looks.
Received from crannies, nooks…
Something staring out at me,
Preventing me from being free.
How do faces show everywhere?
Contorted, mournful, meaning stares?
This cannot be imagination.
Creating fear, constant generation.
Stop looking at me!
Or should I stop looking?
Heavens, I won't stand what that is cooking!
Someone, please save me from this place!
What I thought I withstand; I cannot face.
Please, let there be ways out of the trap!
Please, let this be nothing but crap!
Please, let this be product of an illness!
Please, someone help! I cannot stand the stillness!
I feel this world is meant to scare me.
Why fear bricks, pictures, trees?
Where may I find relief from it all?
When cannot I release fear of The Fall?

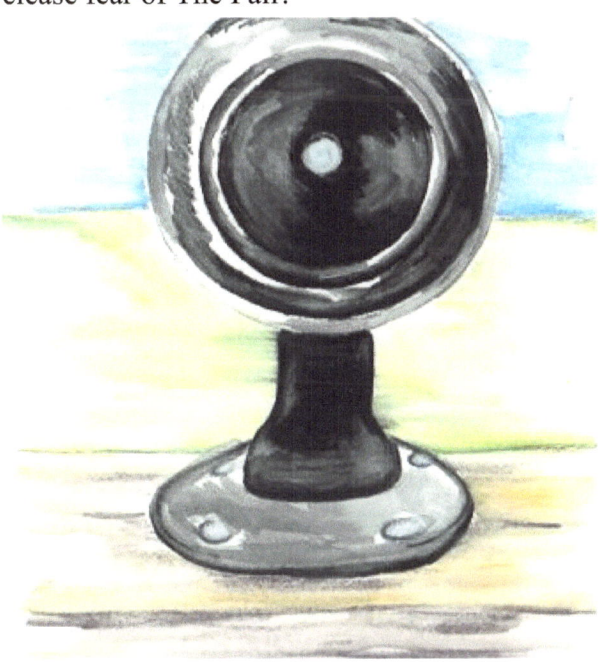

A Decision

How I desire that cigarette…
Seriously, how far did addiction get?
Have one with coffee, ambrosia of the gods.
Calming, soothing, no longer at odds.
Yet, now, forced to hand it over.
Stick up! Criminal! Not leafed clover.
Convince myself: I'll live without them.
But people like me, problems stem.
How many days 'till deadline arrives?
Try not count; do not want to break ties.
The order made; I have to obey.
Others say, right there: my issues lay.
How can I ignore the voice in my head?
Demanding, convincing, claims light it sheds.
All I must do is suffer one loss.
Prove to the Lord He is The Boss.
I cannot run around doing all I want.
This, the reason, surrounded with haunt.
I was self-centered, cared only for me.
Through this letting go, I am finally free.
One thing causing fear: this is a trick?
Will the bad, not good, forever stick?
Still, I will, with hope and prayer…
I cannot become one with that blank stare.
Please take away overwhelmed belief
I had anything to do with "coverage leaf".
Please, through this, am I vindicated?
And future fears completely negated?

Thinking

It is evening and there's rain outside…
I do remember all of those lies.

Thoughts continue, claim "Pinocchio;"
Destiny, the opposite, pleading "No!"

What can I do to make this right?
What must happen to change my sight?

All I see, in life, are my failures.
Seems, to scare me, time has been tailored.

They say I am good, on and on…
Still, I rebut, tell them they are wrong.

Why can't I see good inside me?
Of outside, I'm scared, continue to flee.

Is it because they don't understand?
That really, I am, the baddest of man?

Doubting, looking for reassurance.
No pride in myself, strength as insurance.

It has been this way so long, it seems…
Look to Forever, stifle my screams.

I find no comfort in all I do.
That I knew, is now through.

I ask that He please give a sign.
All I derive: I am not fine.

I apologize, Lord, for being arrogant.
To think I was special – to be Heaven Sent.

Yes, you see some back and forth.
That was the past, not now the course.

With fear, ask: should I be prepared?
For eternity of hardship, an infinity scared?

Please! Do not let the monster get me!
No longer just in the closet, you see?

Creeping up in the people I love!
Giving me glimpses: never-ending shove.

I can write no more at this moment.
My mind has now refused to comment.

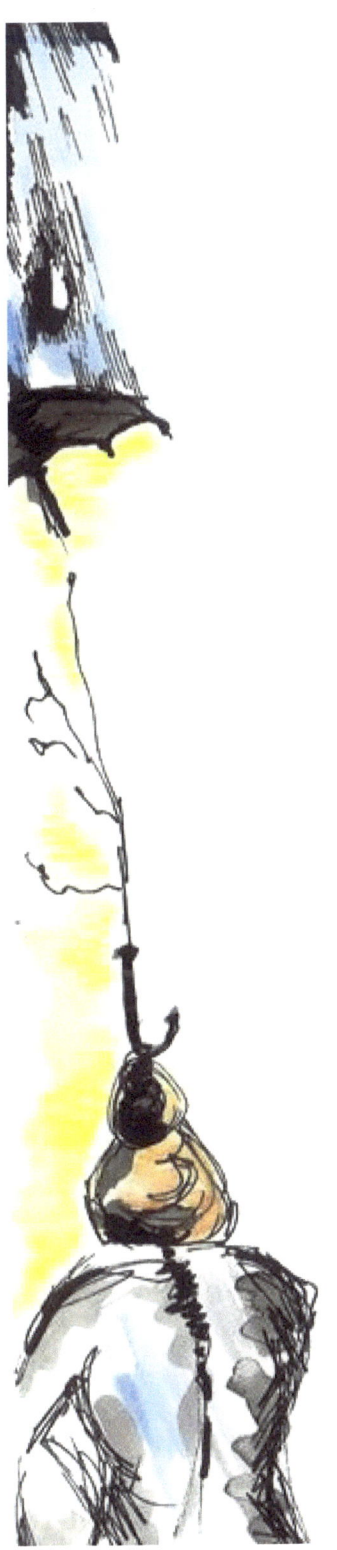

Hide

I need each poem to be the last I write.
Yet, juice does flow, specially at night.

Sometimes, it feels, it is not me writing…
Someone else has control, first nibbles, then biting.

As I said before, I sincerely worry…
Yet now, it seems, the process hurries.

I scare myself out of my wits.
My family then deals with anxiety fits.

What was that? What did you say? What does this mean?
I am slowly, surely, apart at the seam.

However, that might not be bad, you know.
Because, I believe, two may show.

At times, write, did not initiate it.
At times, speak, tongue should be bit.

Multiple personality does not exist, they say.
Please test, I ask… she will come that day?

She does not like me… of that I am sure.
She thinks she is worthy, perfect, and pure.

I am the wrong one, the proverb, bad seed.
I am to blame for every bad deed.

Please extrapolate competition inside.
Allow me to continue good work as I hide.

WAIT! Was that her? Or was that me?
Now, confusion, I know you can see…

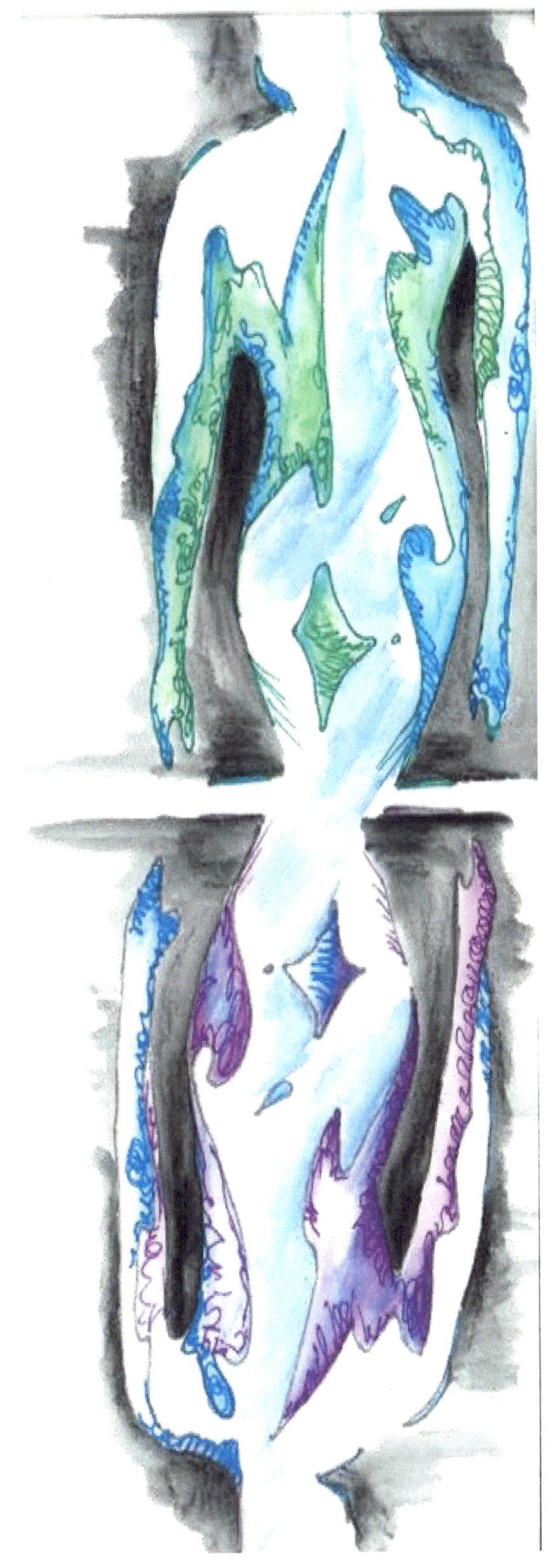

Dear God,

Dear God, I write this poem to You;

Despite You Know, through and through.

At times, I feel, You guide my pen.

Still, I try, doing all I can.

Dear God, I love You, hoping You know.

I see time passed as feeling did grow.

I know the years I went off track;

You know the need to take it back.

Dear God, I am blessed in this life.

Still, this trouble: eye's only sight.

Dear God, I live easier than most.

Sometimes, I feel, through life, I coast.

God, I ask You, love me back…

If You do not, cannot handle that!

I know I sinned, turned dark ways…

Yet, this good in me! I ask it to stay!

Please, do not reject me, as many have.

Fears You will make me utterly sad.

My faith, twisted, completely confused,

The decision I made; I did choose…

Please, Dear God, look at me now.

I came so far; Your Grace allowed.

Please, hold on to me, as I to You;

I am only a person; I know it is true.

You are My Worship, My Reason for Being;

Hope of Your Love fights what I am seeing.

I will battle against the troubles I face.

Devotedly praying, allowed in Your Grace.

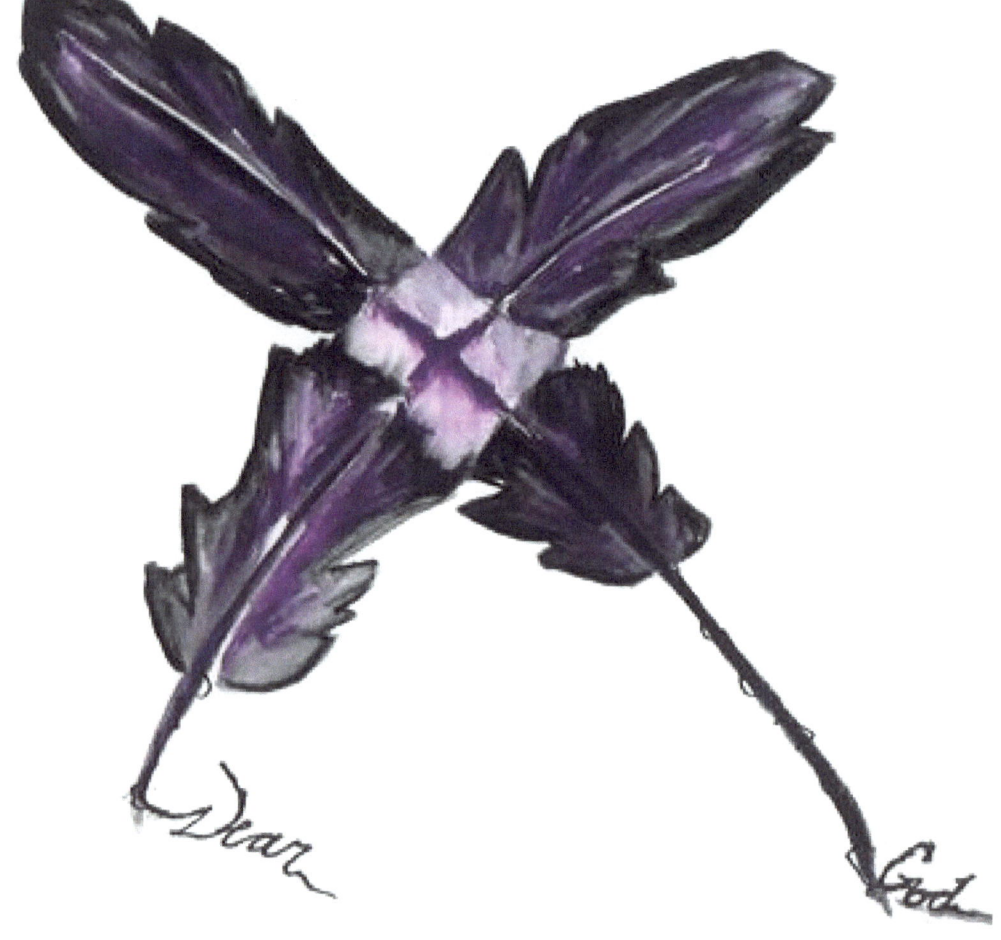

Gone?

Here, I smoke my last cigarette.
Please, tell me, no one took the bet…
One that woke the middle of night.
With ramifications causing fright.

I do love the life You gave me, God.
Though, I admit, they believe I am odd.
I have managed to scare more than a few,
As "psychotic" thought from my mouth did spew.

All I need God, is to be with You;
This "disorder" has set my mind askew.
They tell me: "talk back to the voice,"
I say: "this is result of my choice."

I know, Dear Lord, I was led astray…
Please, let it disappear in this ashtray.
Somehow, still, forward tomorrow…
New life begun, yet with sorrow.

I am scared, God… You are fed up with me?
Am I not the person You meant me to be?
I know I am talent gone to waste.
I know that dark side, I did taste.

Please, Dear God, do not let me go!
I am getting better; progress is slow.
Please, make that voice go far away.
Unless it will help, then it can stay.

I hear repeat: I am not worth it.
Is this what You see? Even a bit?
It surrounds me, chilling my bone.
I know all I face, I face alone.

How can I make everyone see?
Faces, shadow, surrounding me?
When I make it through, will You be Proud?
Or, You will yell? Loudest of Loud?

You are the One who really knows.
All I face here, in the throws.
Please God, let it be for good reason.
Not punishment for an Ultimate Treason.

Those times I had turned the wrong way,
I lost my compass, without mainstay.
I know, I make so many excuse.
My sin, in no way, does this reduce.

Still, Dear God, I need You to see:
Maybe, I am worthy, despite me.
Please, tomorrow, let a new day dawn.
I continue praising You, all days long.

Just please, oh please!
Do not tell me You're gone!

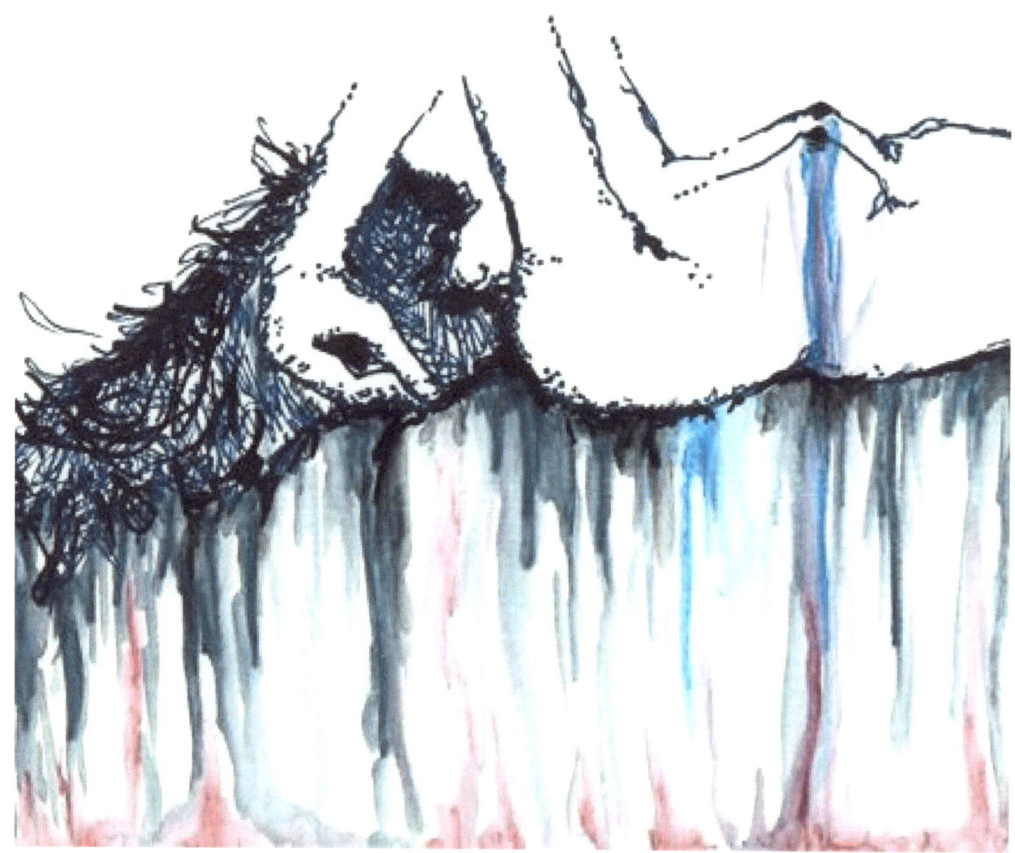

A Push

Decision made to not listen to voice.
Follow my family, they rejoice.

Not knowing if this is right to do.
Feel something, with me, is now through.

Please God, it cannot be someone I love.
Everything different: a push, a shove.

Which way toward, I am not sure.
Still, fear the future, I will endure.

Please

Though I said before
I can write no more...
I fear the last I write.
Dear God, cannot be right!
I tried quitting! I tried to listen!
Stress was too much! Calm was missing!
Please, do not abandon me Lord...
All my love, hope, into You is poured.
I know, I fancy that I can write.
Through this, could my future be bright?
My words, the only talent I offer.
Bringing me pride, the only buffer.
These words are my way to speak to You;
The way I show others their vision is true.
I am so sorry... I could not quit!
Now, I sail this sinking ship.
I need so badly to make You Proud.
Confirming, to You, I do bow.
Please, give time to sort out my faith,
So, You, I can, one day face.
Please, make it so, on that day,
I hold my head up, and at Your Feet lay.
Please, help me fight the scary things.
They are all around; what fear they bring.
I know, I have asked for so much;
Was it real, that night, I saw Your Touch?
Am I special, God? Or I am nothing?
Why should they, my praises, sing?
Why do I believe I belong in the dirt?
Do I know me best? Is that how it works?
How could I possibly find way to ignore?
The constant signs I am only a whore?
Or the voice I hear in their snores?
Is it my lack of completing all of life's chores?
Or is it because I stole that before?
Will there be, for me, Open Door?
I am so sorry; I feel I am chicken...
The monster I see, his lips, he is licking.

I am so scared; I must admit:
On that final day, a failing mark I submit?
I feel responsible for everything wrong,
Yet cannot get to church to sing You a song.
I will stop bothering You, I guess;
Continue to try to do my best.

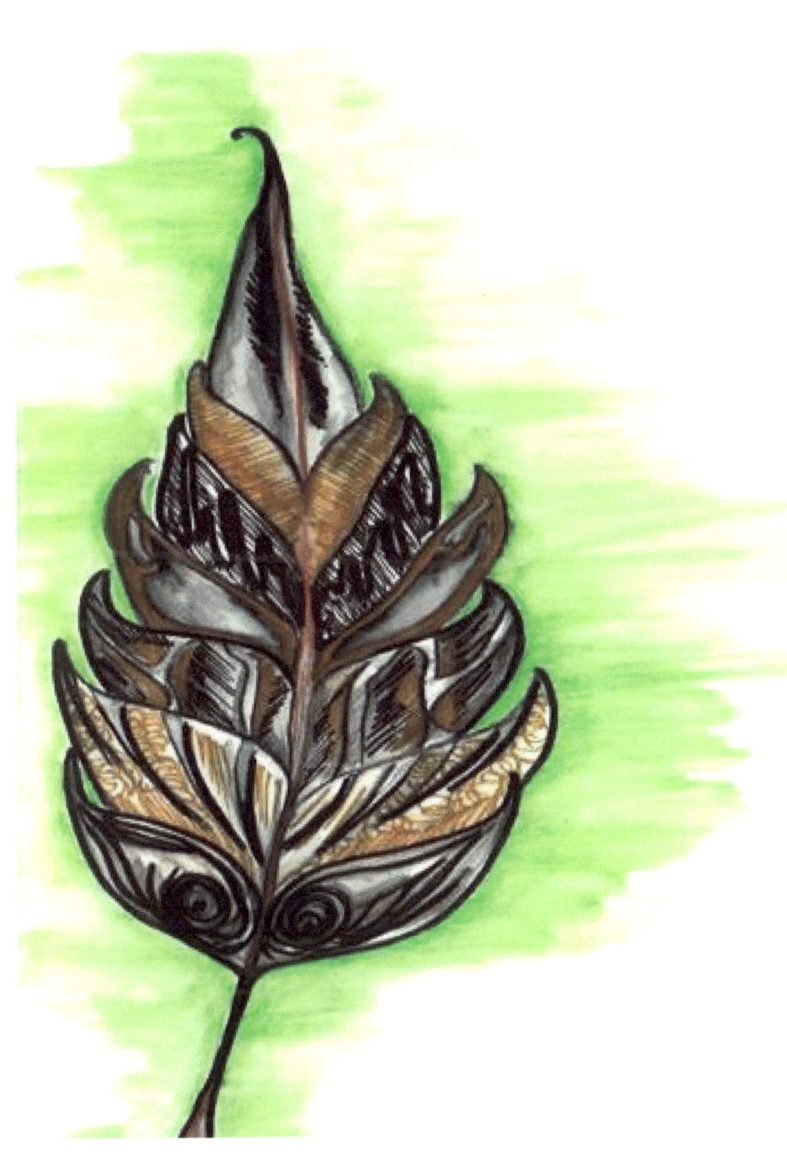

Push and Pull

I used to hear the marching,
Of what, I did not know.
I thought it was the dinosaurs.
Putting on a show.

I was just a child,
Listening to the pillow.
Now, it is here again…
Due to all I owe?

It is difficult to explain:
Certain places I won't go.
I am caught in the headlights,
Frightened rabbit or doe.

I wonder why others
Hands they do not throw?
I am hard to deal with
A line they all must tow.

I am not thankful enough,
Tell how I love them so…
So much to make up for…
More than you'll ever know.

This is what scares me most;
This is the massive blow:
That I cannot correct it all,
Will pay on the day I go?

Please do not let me hear
A huge resounding "No!"
For me, or anyone,
We cannot reap all we sew.

I feel I am an advocate;
Hopeful friend, not foe.
Here, trying to help you all;
Not bring you down below.

Is this the irony?
Is this the Ultimate Snow?
Am I fooling myself?
Is there an Inner Glow?

Please, I cannot be the symbol
Of all wrong with the World…
Please, somehow, affirm for me;
I am always a Good Girl.

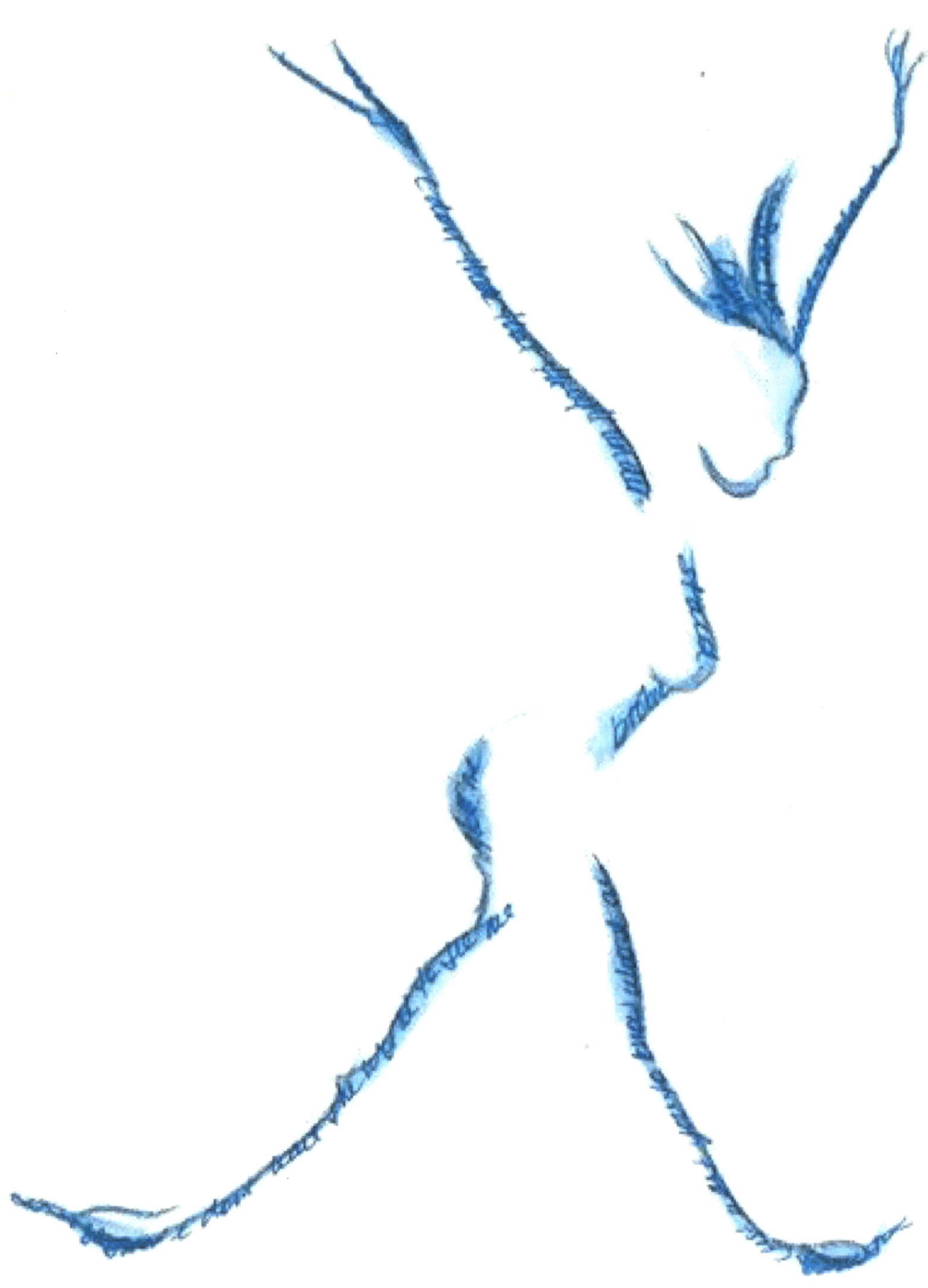

Please, No!

How can it be, every noise, every sound?
Creates fear: what is under the ground?

On the way North, passing River Styx.
Voice in my head: "which did you pick?"

Cars beeping, thinking of the person;
Siren squeal, as I mull, all I have done.

Dogs bark, recalling an old friend;
The Meaning of All: heavy - comprehend.

Hear doors slam, believe it is on me.
Is all this real? Occurs constantly…

Thinking of Hades, hearing a "ding"
Battle, battle, the message it brings.

Fearful of stepping out of the house,
Crows everywhere, hunt me, the mouse.

Dreams culminate, scaring me daily,
Constant reminder of my failing.

They love me, they claim, I will be okay…
God, please let me be, on that day.

It is too hard, pushing through this…
Without kin, am I lost to the abyss?

What will happen when I am alone?
Will anyone hear a frightened moan?

The thought I am a total failure,
Separates me from any saviour.

That voice once said I had lost spirit,
Imagine the laugh… completely satiric.

Is this accurate, correct, right?
Will I not travel into the good night?

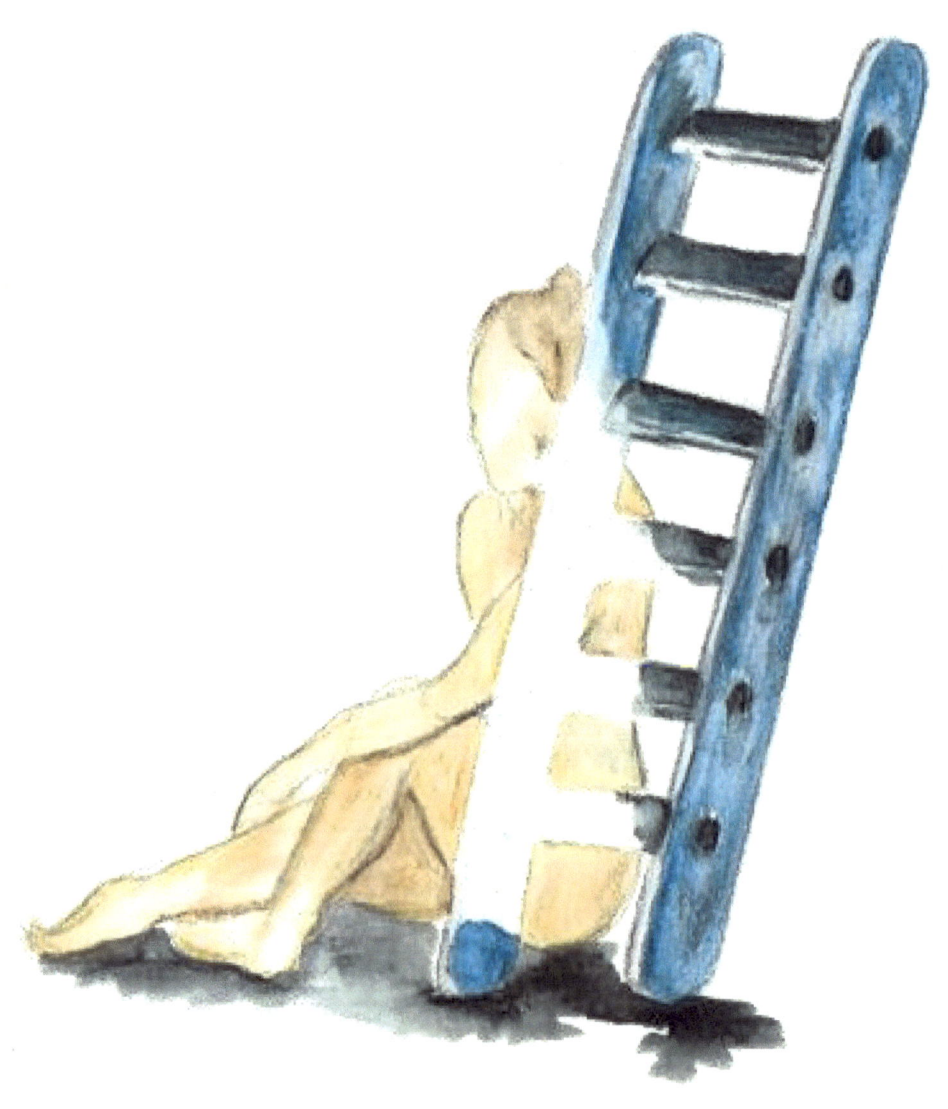

Woe

I am scared he will leave me; I will be all alone?
I am scared he won't hear me; I am only a drone?
I am scared she will pass; no one to talk to?
I am scared I have failed; nothing I can do?
I am scared I am selfish; care only for myself?
I am scared I am a doll; forever on that shelf?
I am scared the dream is real; bad things to come?
I am scared I am not sick; results of all I've done?
I am scared of affirmation of all I fear.
I am scared of that tattoo, beside the eye, a tear?
I am scared I am stupid; perhaps, I am too smart?
I am scared of the bad that maybe I did start?
I am scared each poem only confirms my fate?
I am scared of Destiny and our upcoming date.
I am scared, in the end, of the tears I will cry?
I am scared I did succeed; did I really die?
I am scared I will not end this poem of woe…
At least I was able to let these feelings show.

Letter to All

You have given me life,
I am thankful.
The fear travels deep,
Wish sleep could be restful.

Am I contradiction?
Believing, not worthy?
Am I not allowed in?
Being this nervy?

How could I question?
You and Your Plan?
I must recognize:
A grain of sand.

I know You are Love;
Is my love enough?
How am I this way?
Please make me tough.

Why do I attribute?
Human emotion to You?
Where is my strength?
From all He went through?

God, am I bad?
Do you hate me so?
Is part of you glad?
I learned to grow?

Is all of the change?
Enough in Your Eyes?
Turning the pages,
Part of me has died.

I love you all dearly;
Is this your judgement call?
Do you mock as I am fearing?
The day I may fall?

Forgive all I did
When young or sick.

Release my guilt,
Make life not a trick.

You know how this mind works…
Am I manipulative?
Wanting all of life's perks?
Little effort to give?

Who writes these poems?
You? Is it me?
Do I strike a chord?
Or Your Words I see?

I regret that I had,
Delusions of grandeur…
The wrong I had done,
Caused vision to blur.

I know I did break
So many Commands…
I will correct it all;
Please, give me Your Hands.

I know I did promise…
Temptation got in my way.
So much piling up…
Overwhelming array.

Do I feel empty?
I did not follow through?
From the age twenty…
Behaved as heathens do.

The change: hit thirty;
Look back, in shock.
Too much to handle…
Culminate on spot.

Suddenly, turned,
Facing my past…
Knowing inside:
Fix it, and fast!

A huge part of me:
Always rejected.

What all of you claim:
Completely injected.

Cannot release belief:
Force myself in…
Cannot let go of hope:
I am not full of sin.

I have constant fear:
None of you like me…
That I cannot see
What you know to be?

Am I miserable?
A whiner? A suck?
Are you collecting rocks?
To throw as I duck?

She says: I'm the product
Of years of abuse…
Does not excuse conduct
Or continued drug use!

In life, come a time,
We atone for our sins…
Is this why the rhymes
Creates your nasty grin?

You want me down?
Want me paying a price?
Look at me frown?
Barely notice me twice?

Hate that I am here?
Want me dead and gone?
Glad I suffer fear,
Days, nights, are too long?

To you all: apologies!
Requesting mercy!
Could you oblige?
Lift all the cursing?

I could continue
My letter to you all…

Doubting any of you
Will stop my free fall…

Yet, know, deep inside:
If you were in danger:
I would lift you above
Though you are now stranger.

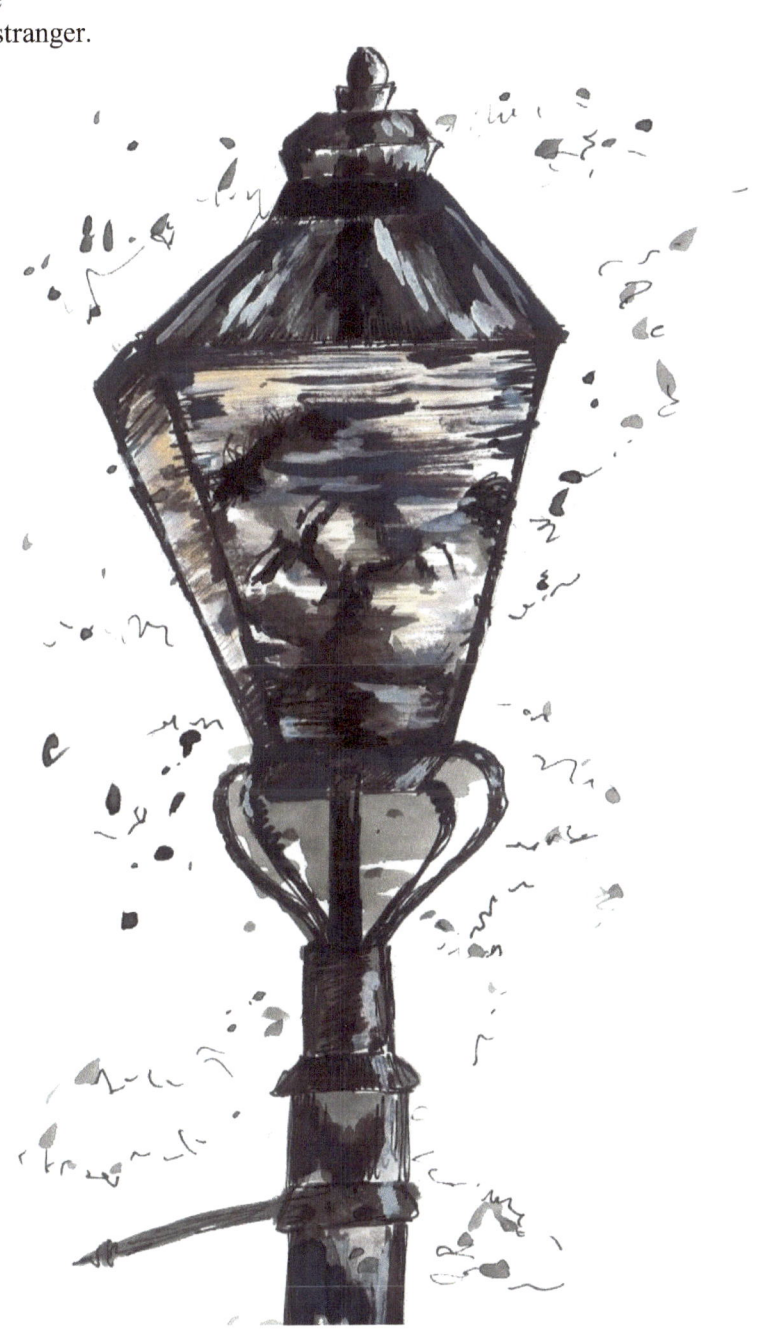

Open the Door

Negativity pulls me down,
Constantly wearing a frown…
Cannot stop hearing sounds,
Can't stop digging up this ground.

I am fearing where I'm bound;
On this door, I have to pound.
Frightening days create a mound;
Knowing why He is crowned.

To You: I have Hope Found.
Pray no enemy, city, town.
Must I trade the white gown?
Could I turn this around?

Please, allow me in Your Grace,
Ever So Profound

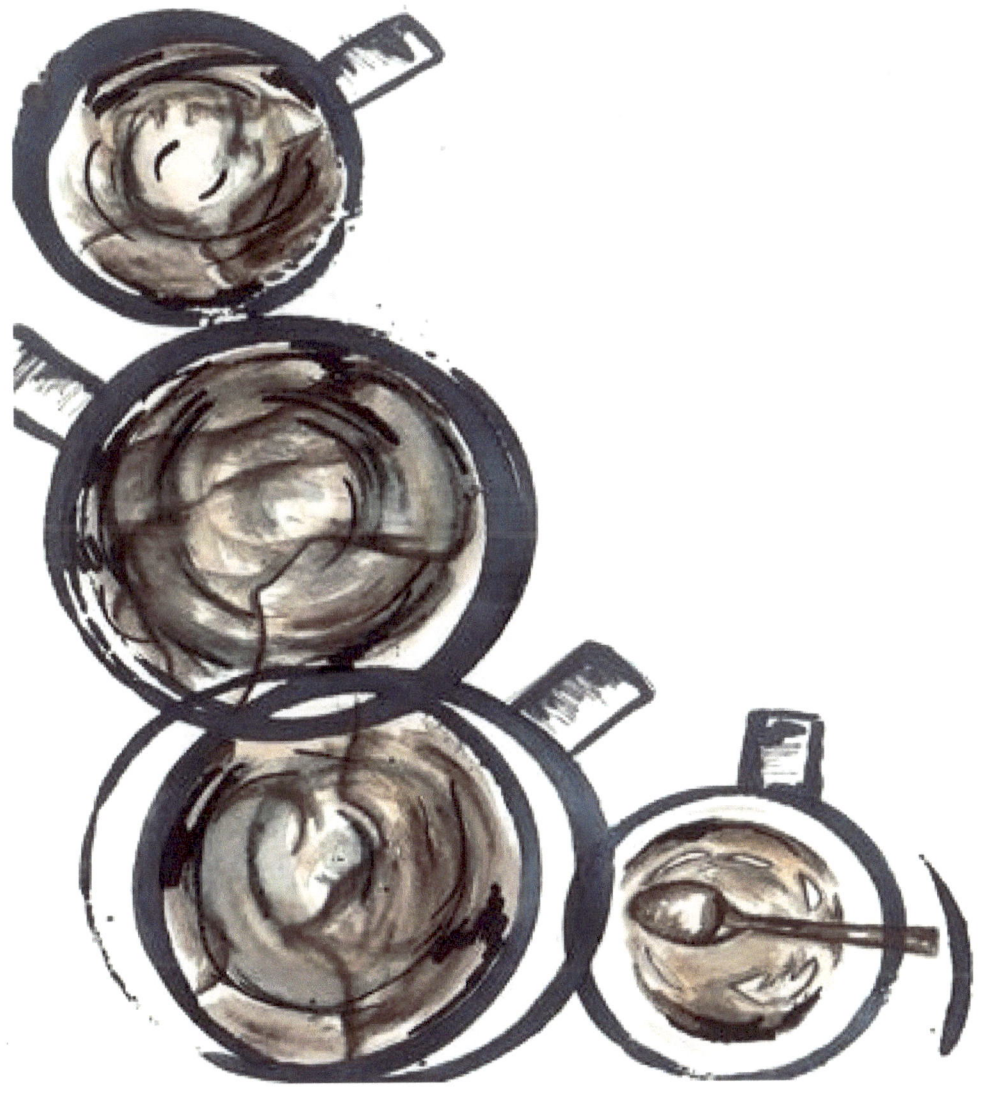

Is Recognition Enough?

I have owned all I have done wrong…
Blew the whistle, sang this song.

He heard me speak my apologies:
Beg for forgiveness; to be set free.

Beating myself up, day in and day out…
Is there any way? Eliminate this doubt?

I do hate myself… I truly do admit.
Sometimes, my reflection, even I forbid.

I am completely and utterly ashamed…
Of all that I had done, the people pained.

Daily, I see, a tiny little light…
Filled with hope: disappears from sight.

At times, I believe those who do love me…
Something then contradicts all they see.

Please, if possible, is my family right?
Could this be an illness? Not Eternal Fight?

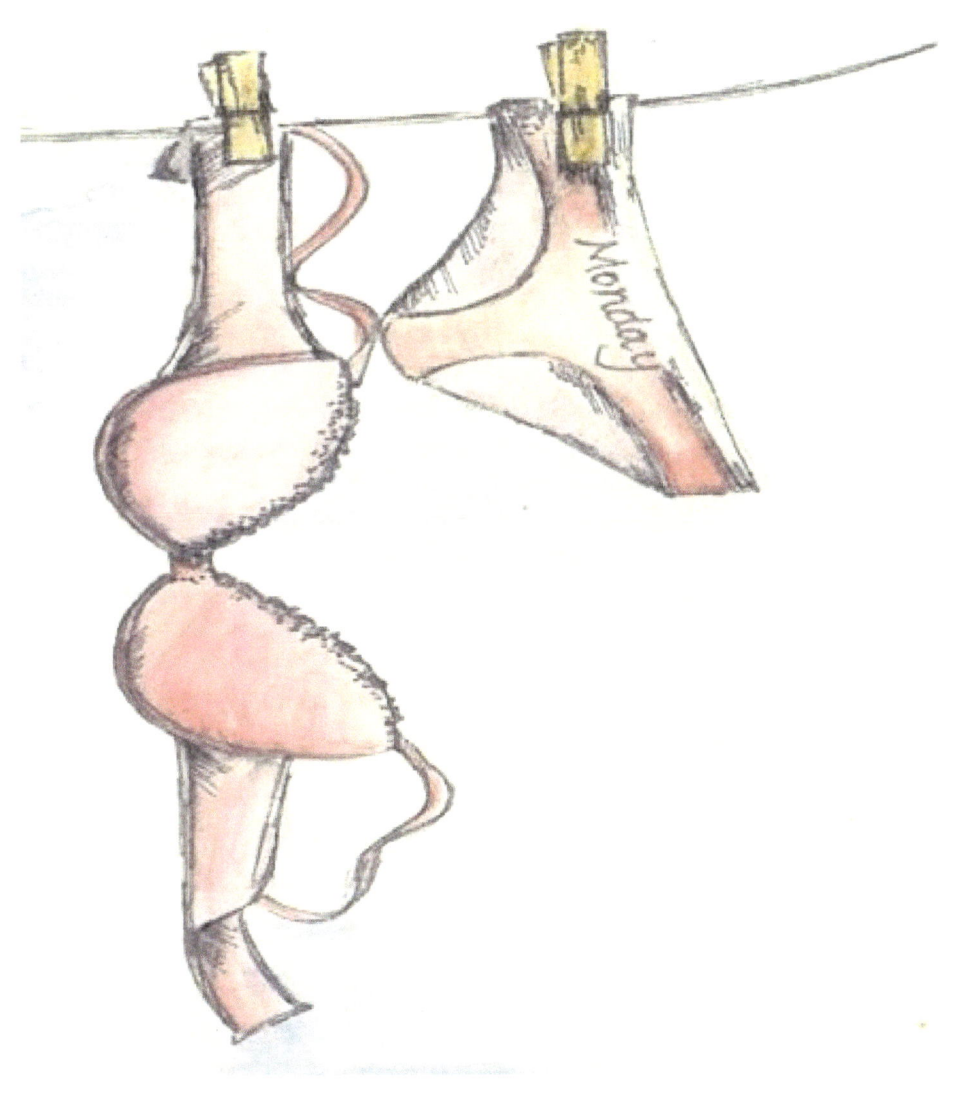

Whose Standards?

This beeping, barking, cawing won't stop!
The message it brings makes my heart drop.
These gurgles, the grunting, normal human sounds
Drove me to a box… "insanity" found.
I tried to describe: message from below!
I tried to explain: this is not a show!
Render me fearful, yet still I stand!
Fighting the thought: with them we land.
All these poems came easily…
Meeting whose standards to a tea?
Now, all continues, raining on me…
Will it extinguish the fire I see?

Trick?

Elizabeth, stop it! Look at yourself!
You are better than this… you do nothing but help!
You will not fall! You will rise above!
Stop being afraid! You know that I love!
I love you, forgive you, and so do they all!
We are watching and waiting… Will anyone fall?
Has anyone repaired all they have done?
Does humanity deserve to garbage be flung?
Do they all look to Me? Begging for love too?
Soon they will learn… perhaps it is true?
You will find a way to let them all know.
Reach up for My Hand, it is you I will tow.

Shock

You have cried all tears you will cry.
Wait and wonder: when will I die?
Are you afraid now? Just ponder and think…
That moment will come. You are on the brink!
Will they stand there and push you over?
Lay in this field… surrounded by clover.
This is going to be quite the show…
Be prepared: they all will know.
You must see: You are NOT worthless.
We will find a way; eliminate the stress.

Someone?

Someone, somewhere, please! Help me?
Please God, please Jesus, do not let this be…
Please, do not let the horrors be true.
Please, could I please, come upstairs too?
Please, do not let the shadows win.
Please, do not throw me to a waste bin.
I love You; I love you; I love you ALL!
Please, oh please, do not let me fall!

Up

Bring people up;
Do not shut down.
You have the ability:
Turn all around.

You have a spark
That we can see…
Seen in the dark;
Believe it can be!

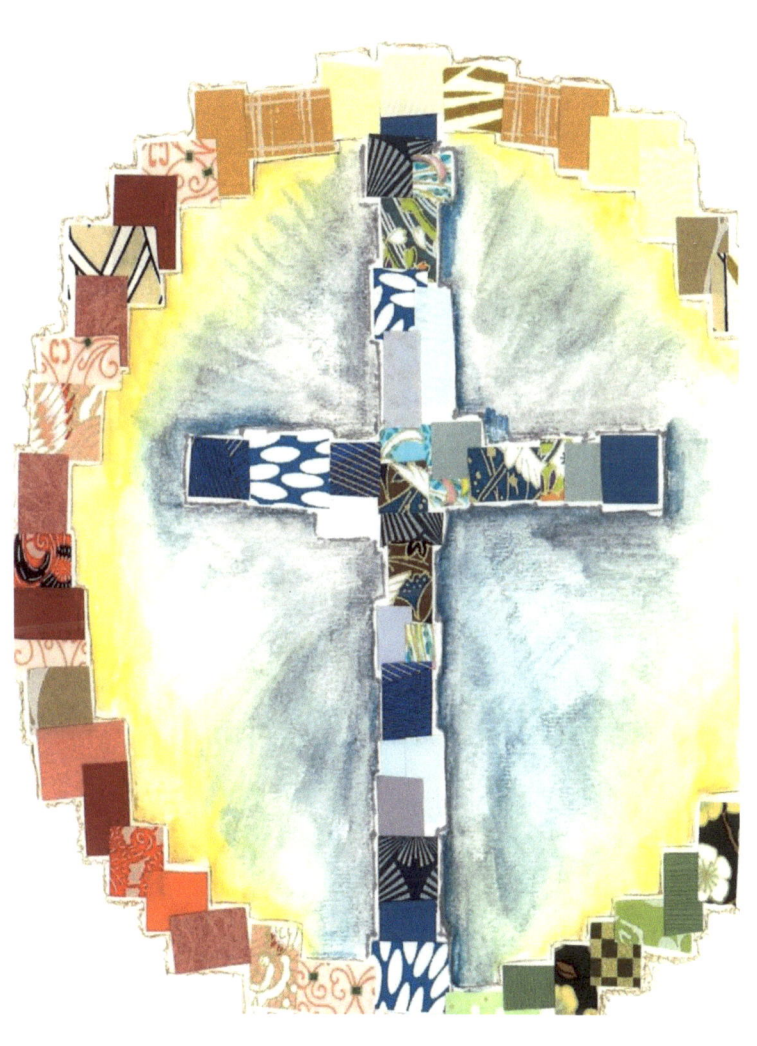

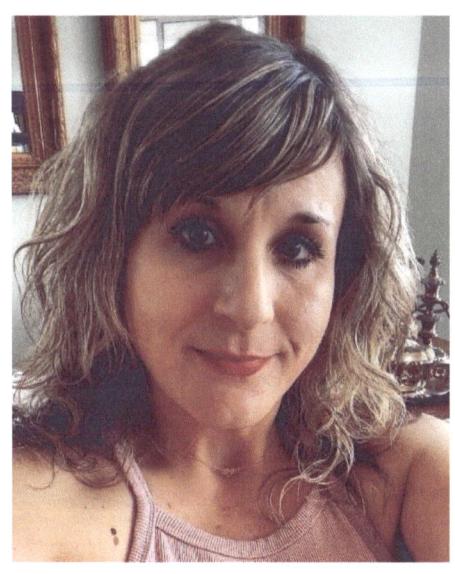

Elizabeth Weseloh (Poet):

Elizabeth's poetry delves deep within herself and is intended to evoke emotion in the reader. It is Elizabeth's hope that her writing will engage and enlighten the audience, while offering opportunities for self-reflection.

Please visit Elizabeth's website at www.poetrybyelizabeth.com and her Instagram @miss_elisabete

Michelle Heitzner (Illustrator):

By applying painting, mixed media and abstraction, Michelle seduces the viewer into a world that articulates the beauty around, and within us.

Please visit Michelle's website at: www.artistmich.com and her Instagram @artistmich

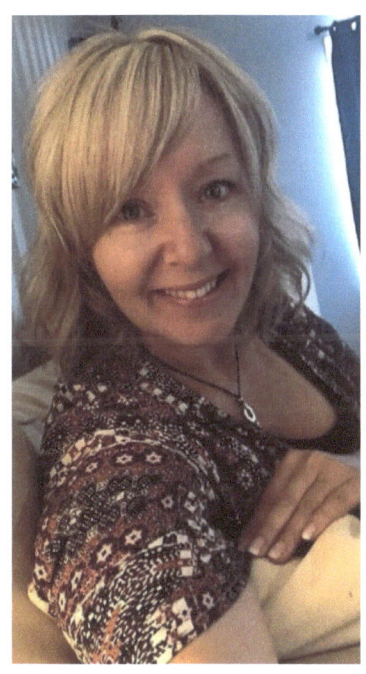

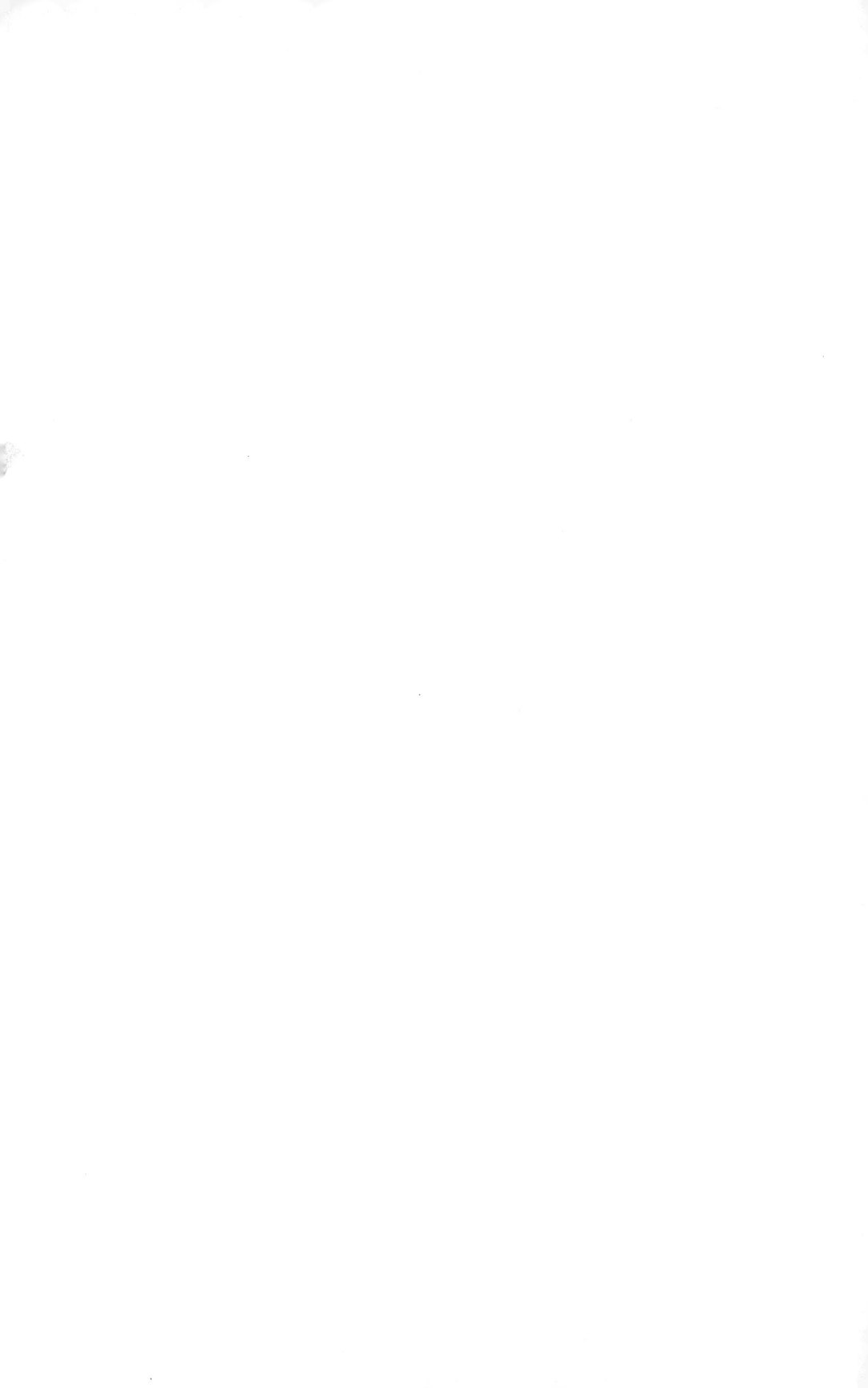

www.ingramcontent.com/pod-product-compliance
Lightning Source LLC
Chambersburg PA
CBHW040327220526
45473CB00009B/2588